THE JIM THOMPSON HOUSE

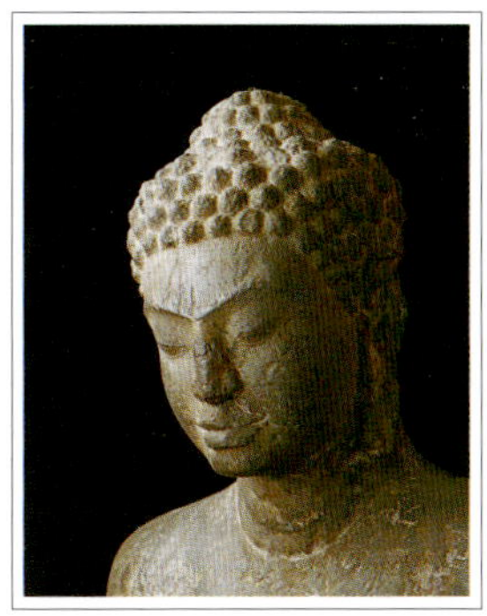

Text by WILLIAM WARREN

WITH A CONTRIBUTION ON THE ART COLLECTION BY

JEAN-MICHEL BEURDELEY

Photographs by LUCA INVERNIZZI TETTONI

THE JAMES H.W. THOMPSON FOUNDATION

EDITIONS DIDIER MILLET

Down a narrow, nondescript Bangkok lane, the graceful red roofs of a traditional Thai residence rise above a lush tropical garden, in serene contrast to the city's modern clamor all around. This was the home of an American named Jim Thompson, and it stands today as a continuing memorial to a remarkable man and to his love for Thailand's rich culture.

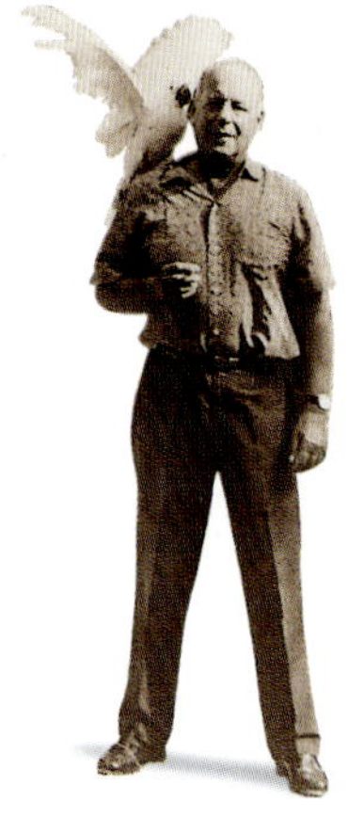

Above: Jim Thompson and his pet cockatoo, Cocky.

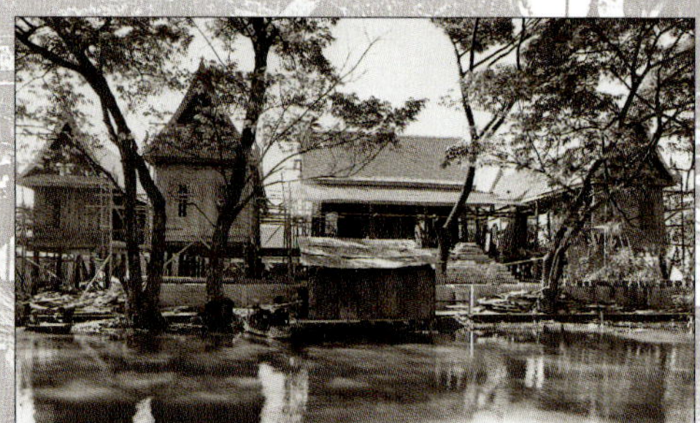

Left: The Jim Thompson house under construction, end of 1958. The main house departs from traditional Thai architecture in several ways. The house faces the canal, as most Thai houses do, though visitors have always arrived at what is actually the rear entrance.

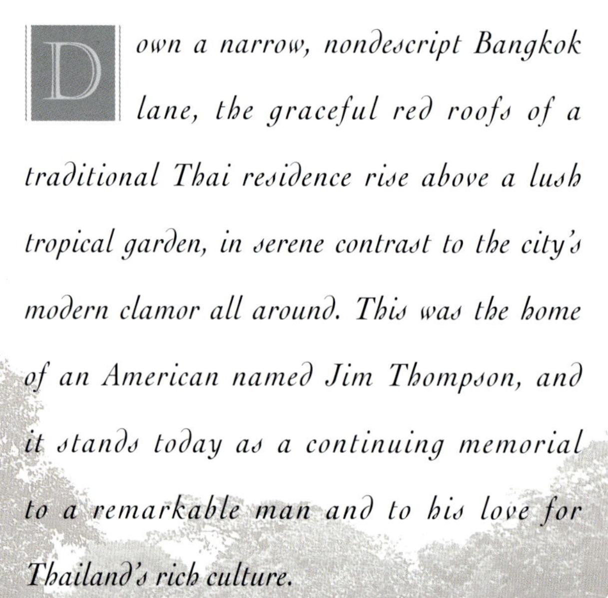

Right: Overview of the Thompson house and the courtyard entrance.

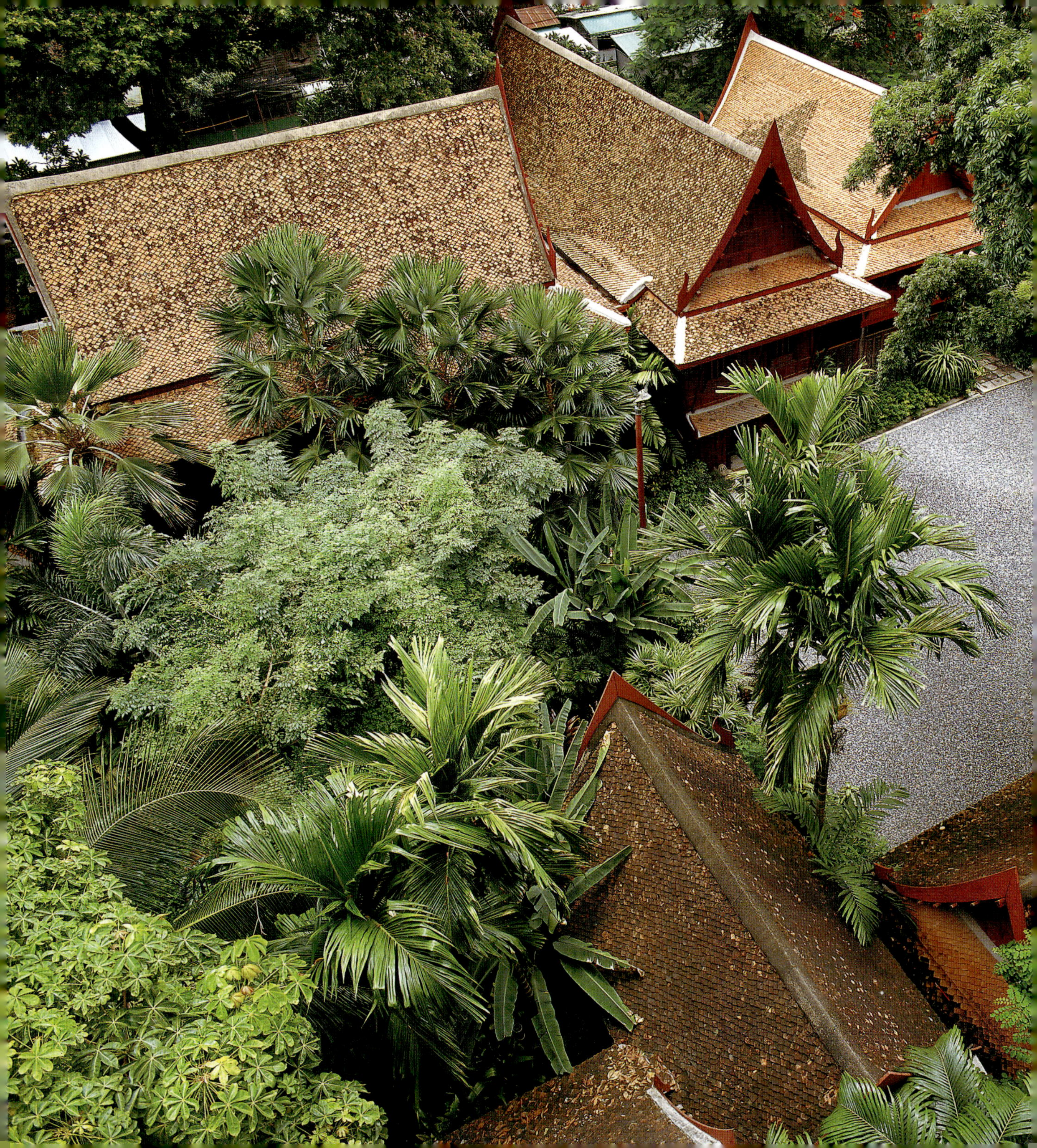

The Man

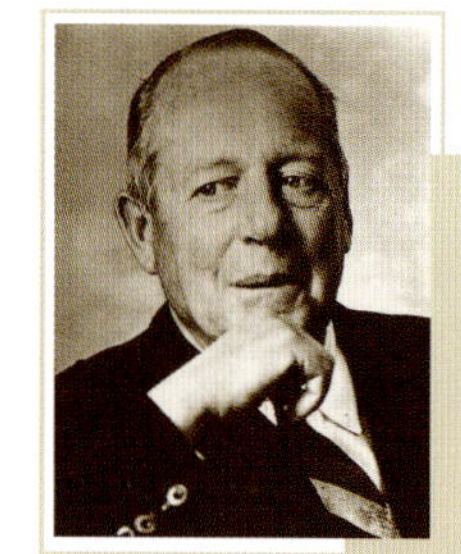

Top: Jim Thompson, the self-made successful American businessman.

Below: Thompson inspecting new silk pieces at the klong side. In the late 1940s, there were only a few weavers left in Bangkok, mostly in an old section called Bang Krua, as well as others scattered about in villages of the north and northeastern regions. With the revival of the industry by Jim Thompson, more and more Thais went back into silk rearing and weaving.

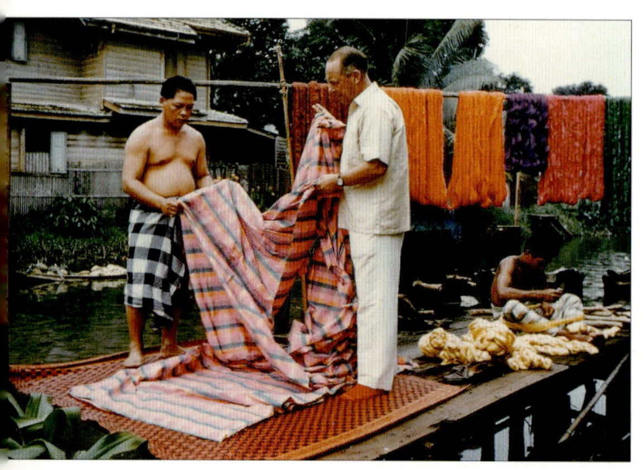

Nothing in James H.W. Thompson's early life suggested that he would find fame and contentment in such an exotic setting. Born in Greenville, Delaware, in 1906, he was educated at St. Paul's, Princeton, and later at the University of Pennsylvania. He worked as an architect in New York until the beginning of the Second World War, when he enlisted in the army.

During the war, Thompson worked with the Office of Strategic Services (OSS), and it was in this capacity that he came to Asia as part of a group scheduled to parachute into Thailand. When Japan surrendered in August 1945, he arrived in Thailand by more conventional means, just two days after the end of hostilities. The beauty and friendliness of the country and its people immediately appealed to him, and, upon receiving his discharge from the service, he decided to settle down and make it his home.

After working for a year or so on a project to restore the old Oriental Hotel, his

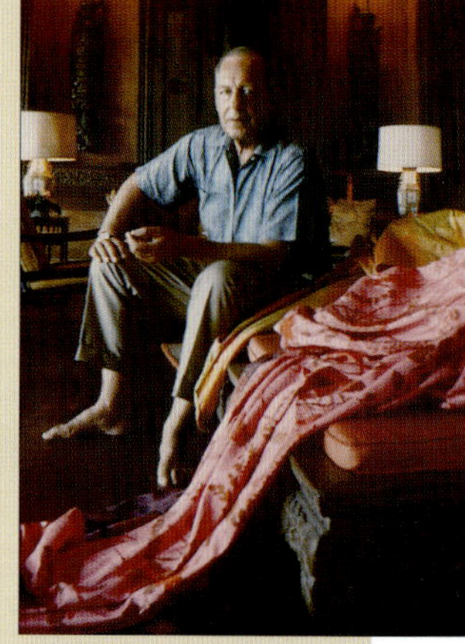

Above: Jim Thompson displaying some of his silks in the drawing room of his house.

Right: Her Majesty, Queen Sirikit and Thompson in his first silk shop.

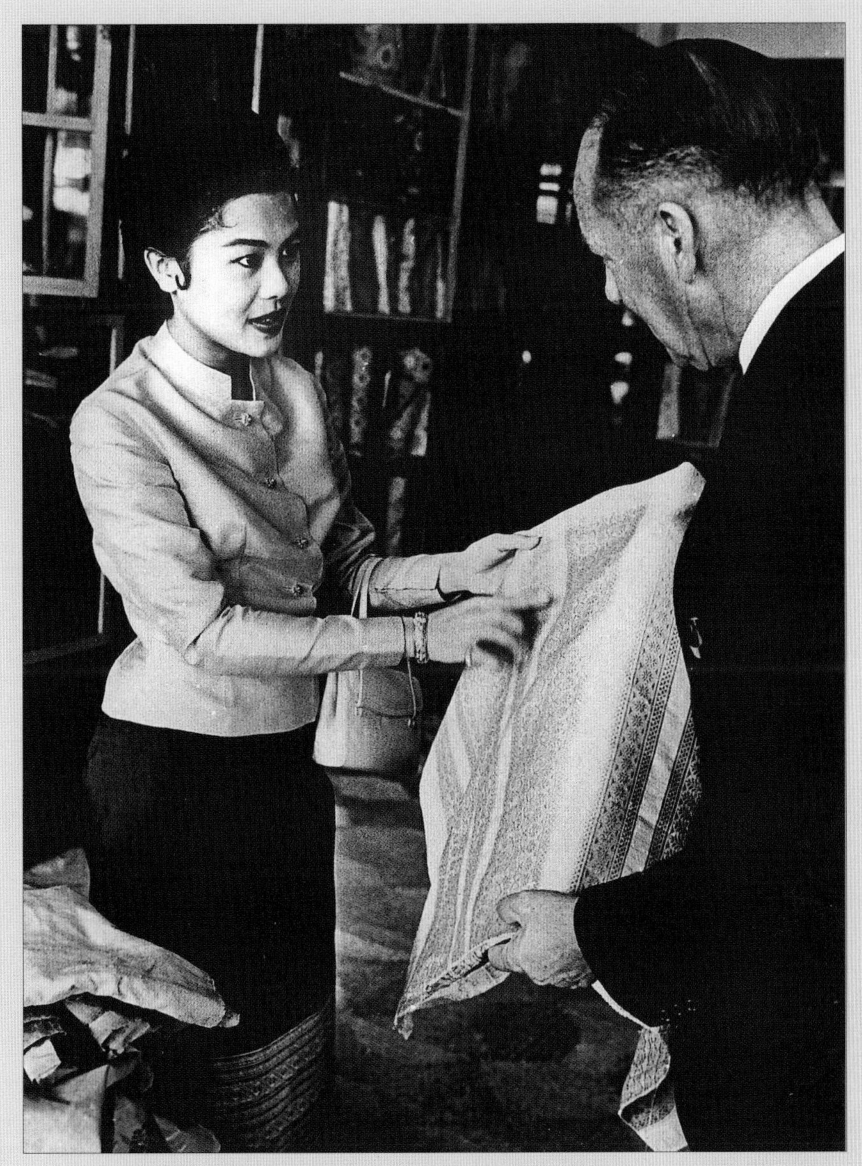

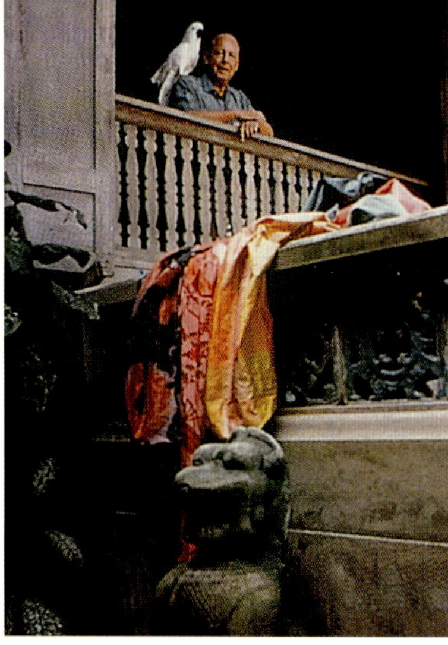

Above: Thompson and his pet cockatoo, Cocky, standing on the verandah of his house.

Below: Pieces of the brightly-colored Thai silks that have so successfully captured the fashion world's attention.

interest turned to the commercial possibilities of Thai silk, an ancient handicraft that was fast disappearing due to competition from cheaper, machine-made fabrics.

Convinced that the beauty and quality of the material would have an appeal outside Thailand, Thompson assembled a small collection and took it to show friends in New York. There the response was sufficiently enthusiastic for him to return to Bangkok and, with a group of shareholders, start the Thai Silk Company, Ltd.

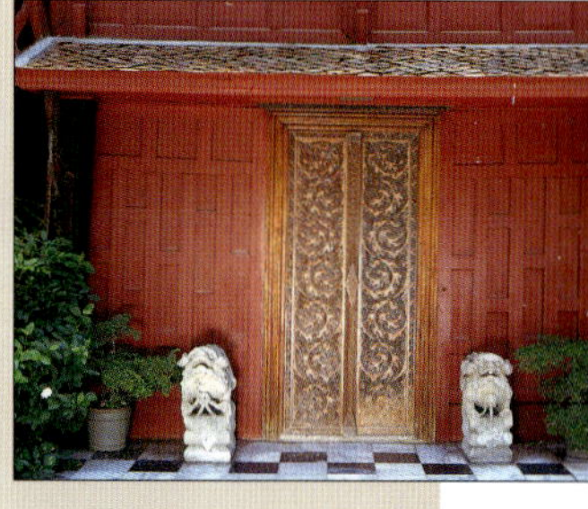

The ornately carved teak doors leading to the entrance hall of the house are flanked by two 19th-century Chinese stone lions.

The business was by no means an overnight success. There were technical problems to overcome—the introduction of color-fast chemical dyes, for instance—but Thompson's confidence and commitment attracted more weavers and steadily more customers. A major turning point was the decision to use Thai silk for costumes in "The King and I", both on the stage and in the film version. Fashion designers and interior decorators were also attracted to the shimmering fabric, and exports, as well as local sales, began to expand. By the 1960s,

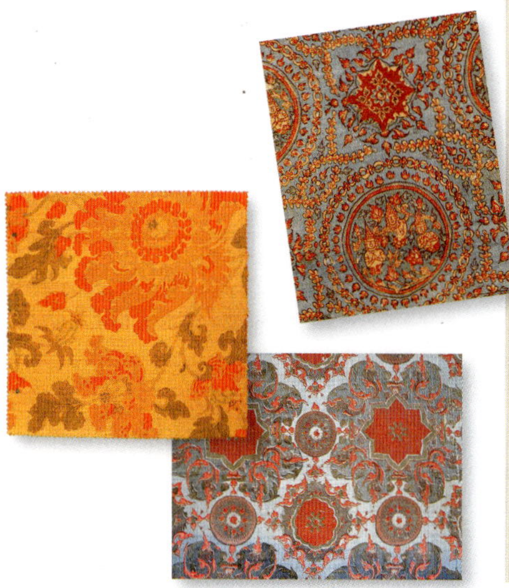

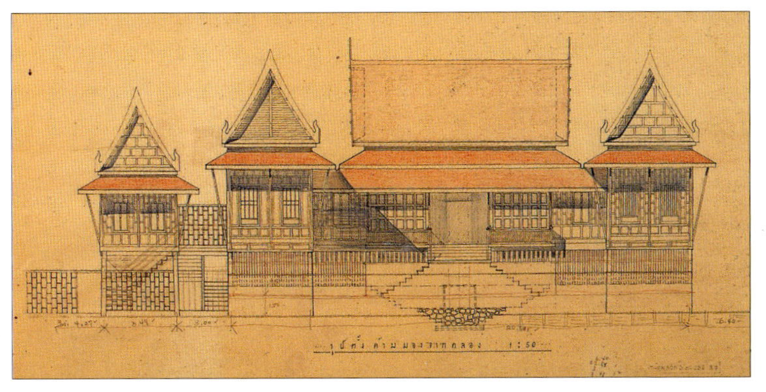

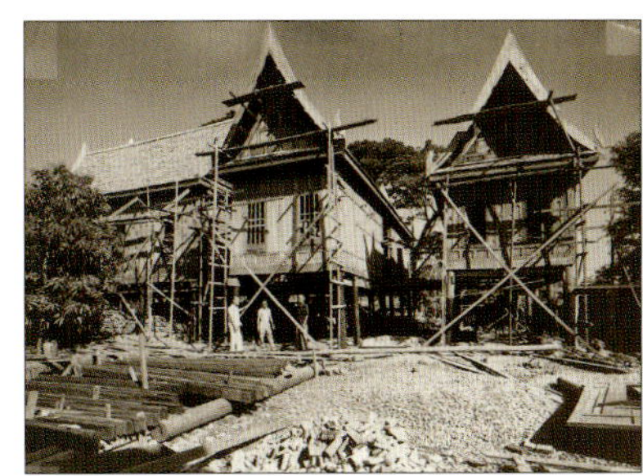

Above: The original architectural drawings for the Jim Thompson house, prepared by Thompson and a Thai architect, differ in a number of respects from the completed house. During construction, builders from Bangkok proved to be unfamiliar with traditional techniques and carpenters had to be brought from Ayutthaya.

Above right: The house under construction, early 1959. The various structures used to assemble the residence came from as near as the weaving community across the canal and from as far as the old capital of Ayutthaya.

there were over a hundred other silk companies in Thailand, giving employment to thousands of Thais, and silk had become perhaps the country's most famous single product.

At the same time, Thompson was also becoming increasingly interested in Southeast Asian art and domestic Thai architecture. These two interests were memorably combined when he built the famous residence featured in this booklet.

In March 1967, Jim Thompson went for a holiday with friends to the Cameron Highlands, Malaysia. There, he presumably went for a walk in the surrounding jungle and never returned, leaving behind an enduring mystery.

Below: Both the supporting columns and, consequently, the walls of the house lean slightly inward, adding to the illusion of height and grace. The curved roof-ends, characteristic of traditional Thai houses, are probably adaptations of naga (serpent) motifs.

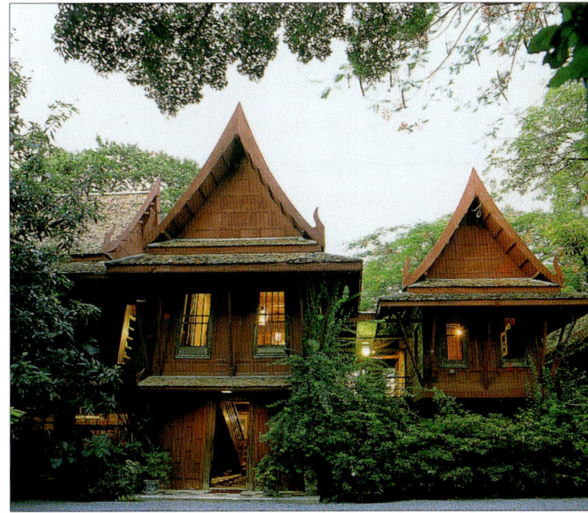

The Garden

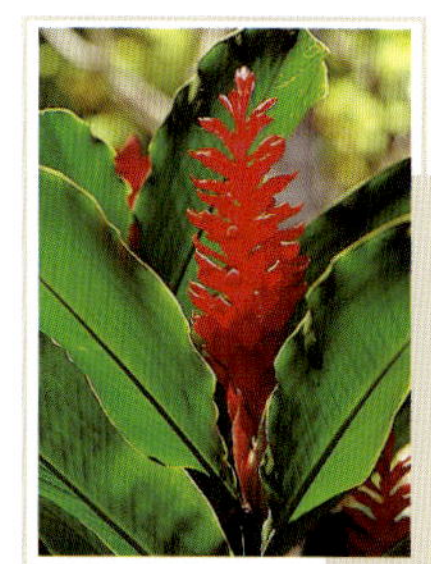

In a letter to his sister while he was still drawing up plans for his house, Jim Thompson indicated the garden area as "jungle". This reflected his preference for an informal, somewhat wild looking landscape, and that is what a visitor sees today. Taller specimens like palms, ficus, flowering bananas, flame of the forest, and rain trees rise above a dense planting of tropical ornamentals with varied leaf textures and colors as well as flowers.

A characteristic of most tropical gardens is that growth is more or less continual, especially during the rainy season, and original landscape designs are soon obscured. The Jim Thompson garden has, thus, often changed over the more than thirty years since he lived there, with new plants being added and older ones removed. The atmosphere, however, remains the same—a "tame jungle" that constantly surprises with unexpected views and exotic specimens unfamiliar to many temperate gardens.

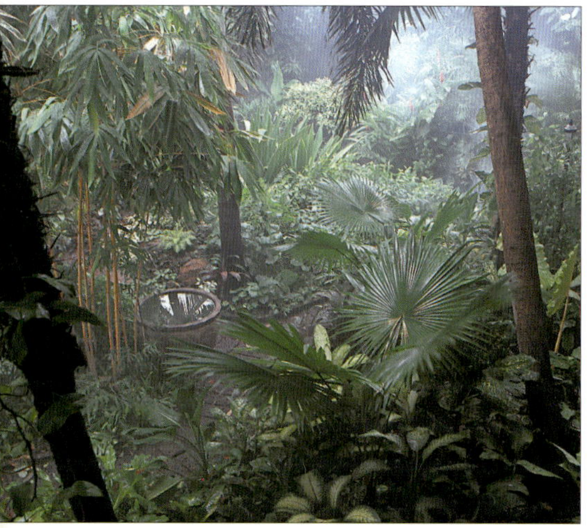

Top: *Alpinia purpurata*, the red ginger.

Above: A view of the garden from the open area below the house; palms, golden bamboo, and other ornamentals provide a variety of textures and colors.

Right: A view of the side garden from the master bedroom; on the left is a house now used to display textiles.

Below: The spirit house, symbolic residence of the guardian who watches over the compound.

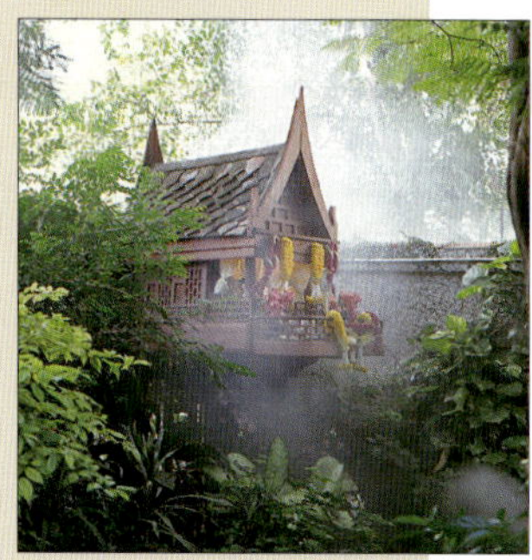

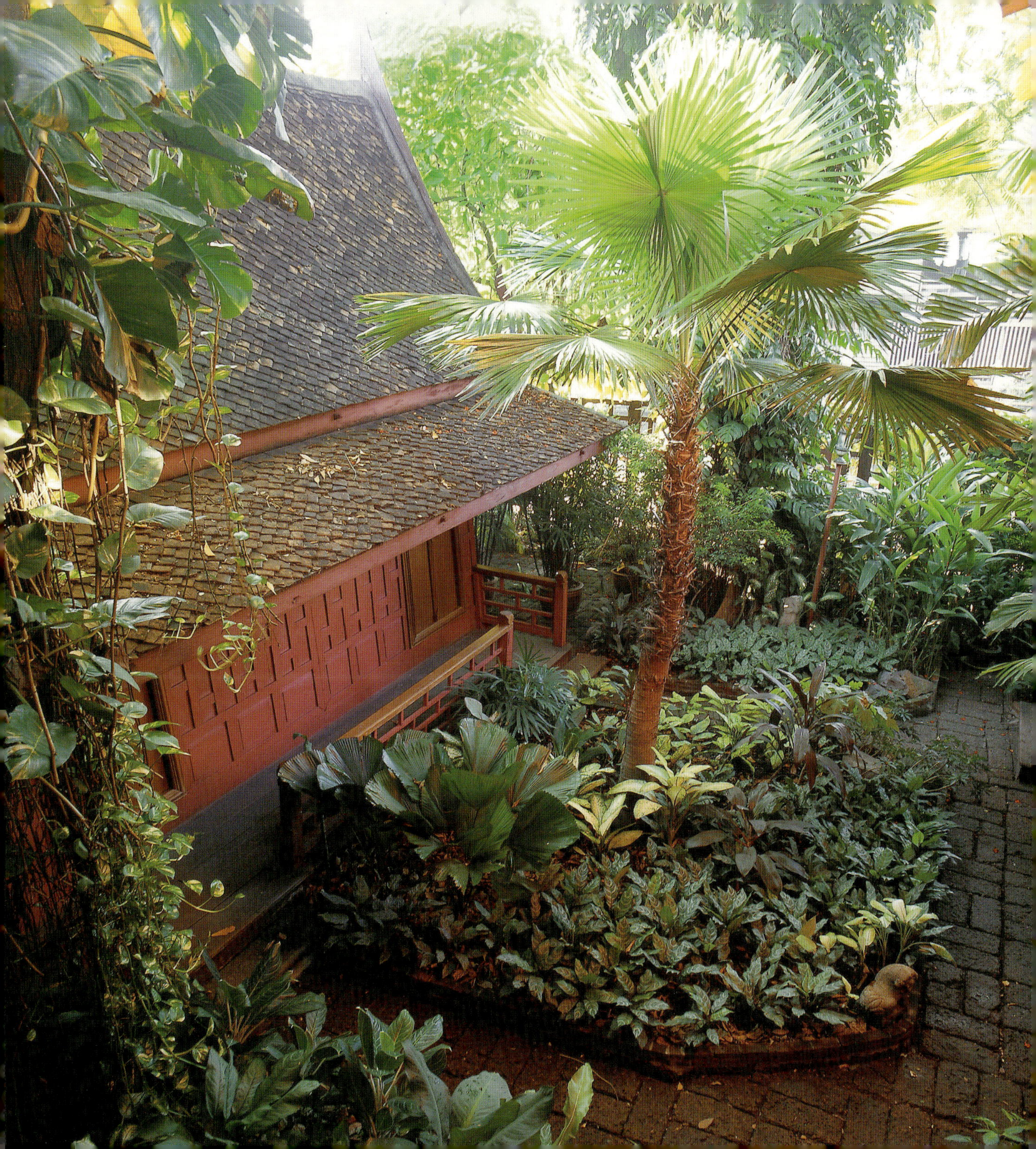

the house

The House

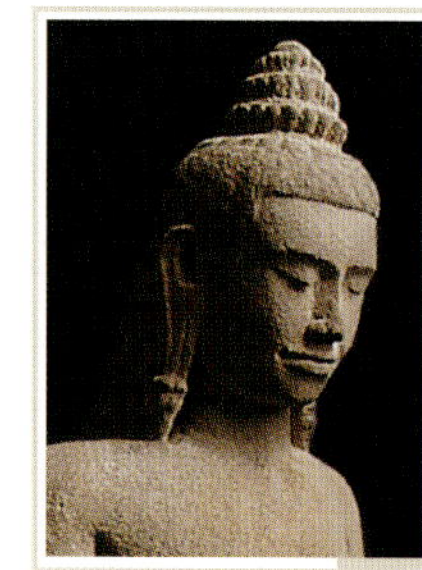

Above: Head of a seated Buddha displayed on the upper landing. The sandstone statue, 81.5 cm high, belongs to the Lopburi school, 13th century and was found in Suphanburi Province, Thailand.

Below: Painting on wood from the life of the Buddha, early 20th century; a note on the back identifies the painter as Lerts Siana.

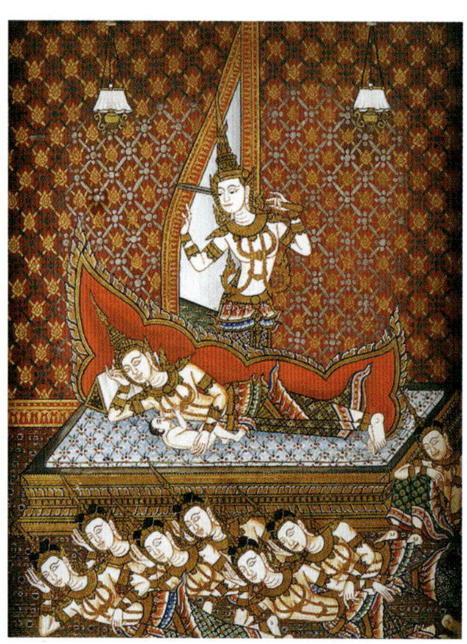

More subdued than the glittering palaces and temples that enchant visitors, Thailand's traditional houses are at once elegant and eminently practical. Hard, long-lasting teak was the preferred material and the whole structure was raised from the ground on stout columns, thus providing protection from floods and wild animals. The area underneath the house was also a convenient place to keep family livestock, store crops, and undertake cottage industries like silk weaving. Steep roofs and broad overhangs protect the interior from the elements, while most group activities take place on a breezy central platform.

There are few purely decorative touches on a Thai house. The most striking are the bargeboards that rise to a sharp peak in the middle and curve upward at either end, the panelled walls, and the carved panels below the windows and above the doors. Raised thresholds may have a symbolic purpose in keeping evil spirits from entering the rooms but also strengthen the walls structurally.

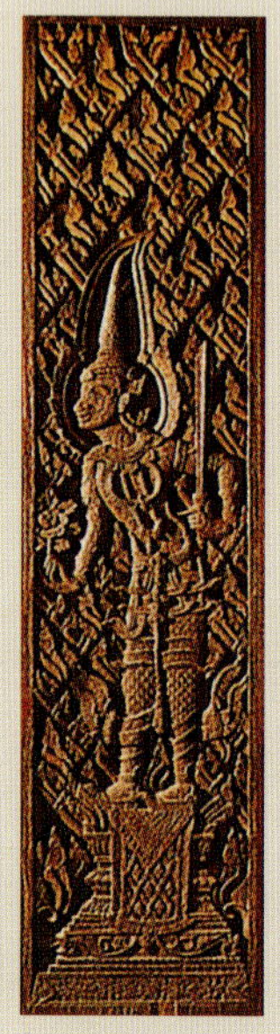

Above: One of two carved teak doors leading to the rear of the entrance hall, early 19th century, showing a guardian deity.

Right top: The terrace of the Jim Thompson house, arranged for a party.

Right bottom: Chinese porcelains in a cabbage-leaf pattern and a tray holding traditional Thai flower arrangements.

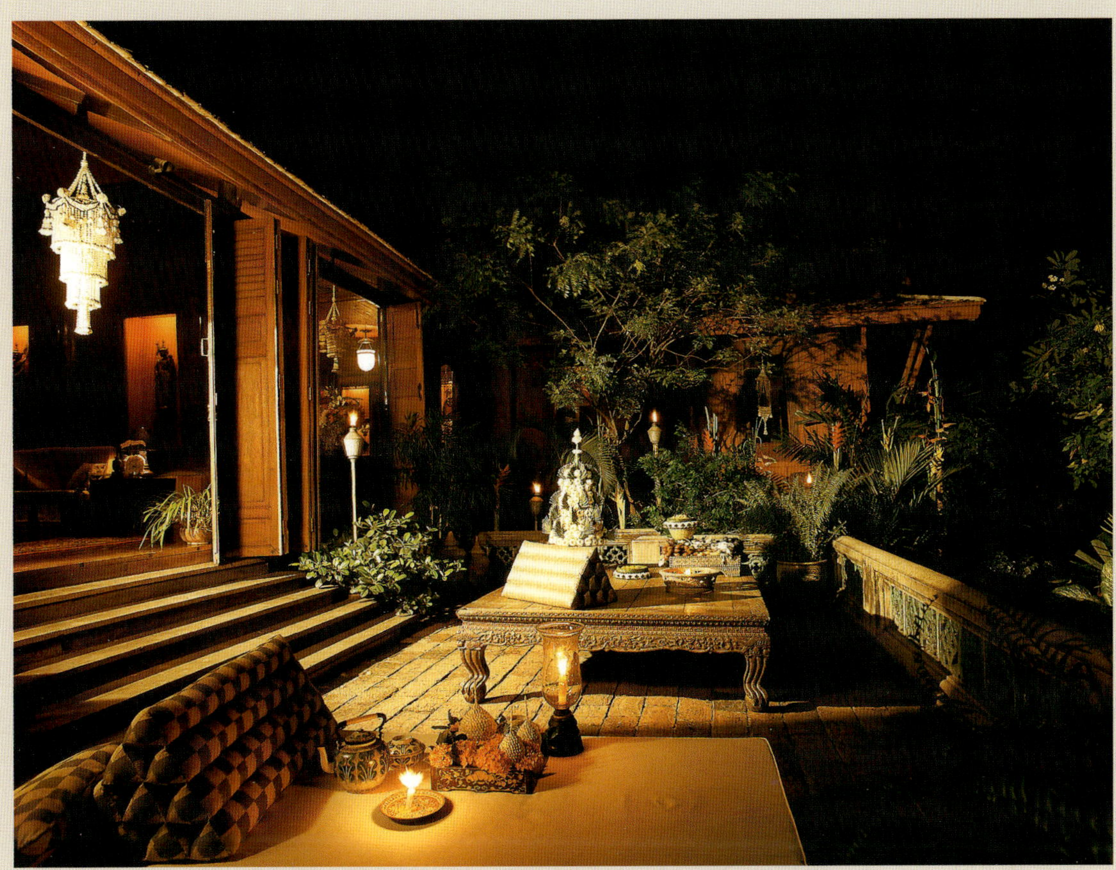

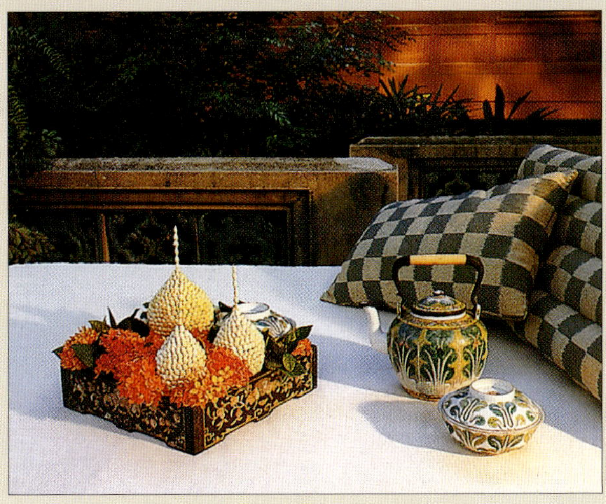

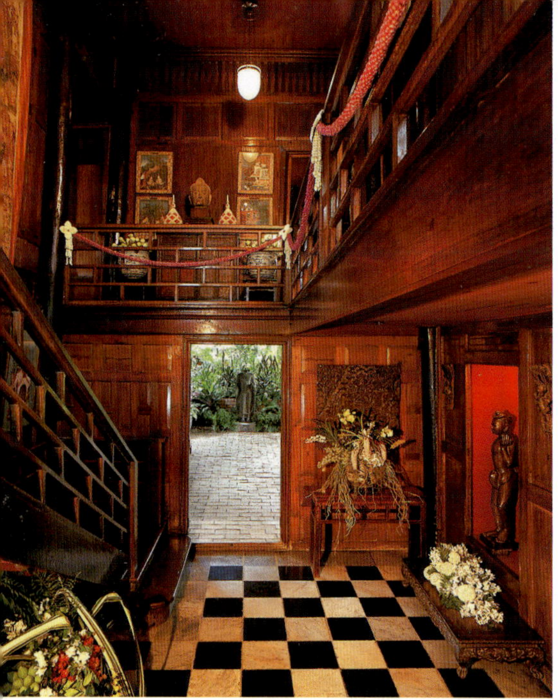

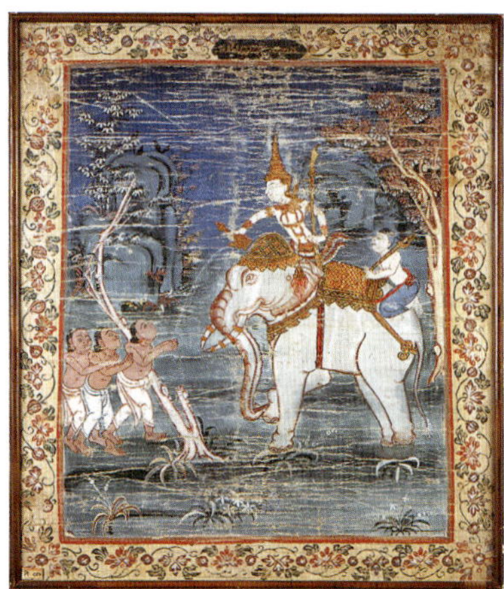

Above: Scene from the Vessantara Jataka showing Prince Vessantara giving away his precious white elephant.

Work on the house began on 13 September, 1958 and was officially completed on 3 April, 1959. In between, three important rituals were held. The first took place when the initial wooden pillar was raised and was presided over by nine Buddhist priests. The second involved finding a suitable location for the spirit house, symbolic residence of the Phra Phum, or guardian spirit, who watches over that particular piece of land. The final ceremony, by far the most important, marked the official completion of the house; nine priests participated, during which prayers were chanted and lustral water was sprinkled to bless the premises.

The Entrance Hall

Although it is architecturally at the rear of the house, visitors to the Jim Thompson house arrive by way of the lofty entrance hall, which rises two floors and includes both the staircase and the upper landing on two sides. Buildings to form this section came from a village called Pak Hai, northwest of Ayutthaya, while the black and white marble

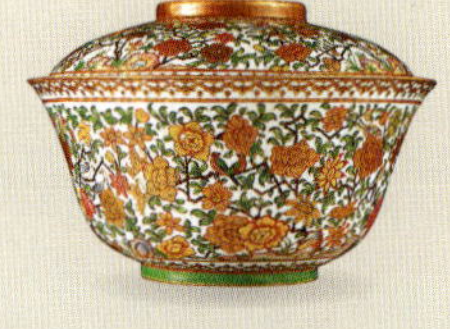

Bencharong bowl. Wares like this were made in China for export to Thailand, often using Thai designs.

Top left: The entrance hall. In the niches on the right, a standing Buddha of the Ayutthaya school and a Burmese boy representing a gong carrier are displayed.

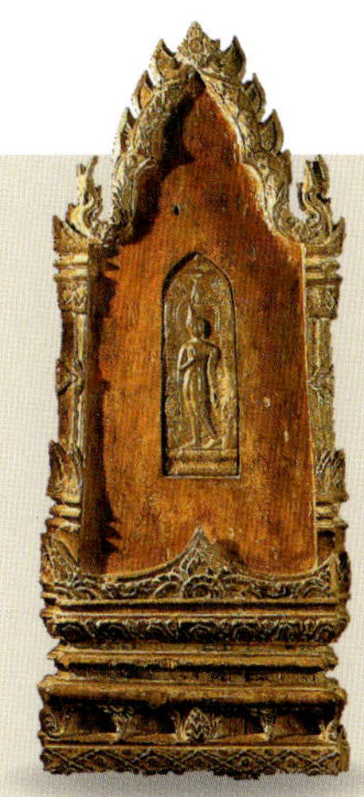

Above: Bronze votive plaque, 31 cm tall, showing the Walking Buddha, a notable creation of the Sukhothai period. This kind of image remained popular in the next capital of Ayutthaya, where this was probably made in the 14th century. The wooden frame also came from Ayutthaya Period.

Right: Limestone figure of Siva, the greatest of the earthly Hindu gods, 59.5 cm tall, Lopburi school, 12th century. It came from the northeastern part of Thailand, Surin province.

Right bottom: Limestone figure of the Hindu goddess Uma, 60.5 cm tall. Like the Siva figure on the left, it could be classified as Lopburi school, 12th century and came from Surin province.

floor tiles came from a Bangkok palace. The bowl-shaped lighting fixture was also typical of aristocratic homes in the late nineteenth century.

Framed in the doorway at the end of the hall is a torso of the Buddha in sandstone from the Dvaravati School, late seventh and early eighth centuries, which came from Lopburi Province in central Thailand. A Thai standing Buddha and a carved pediment panel hanging in the entry way are Ayutthaya style.

Particularly striking, in the hall and elsewhere in the house, is a large collection of traditional Thai paintings, generally on cloth but some on paper and wood. These were done by anonymous priest-painters or commissioned laymen as acts of religious devotion rather than of conscious artistic creation and were originally intended as aids in religious instruction. The subjects of most are the life of the Buddha (the large, tapestry-like paintings along the staircase, for example) and the moralistic Jataka stories depicting the Buddha's previous lives.

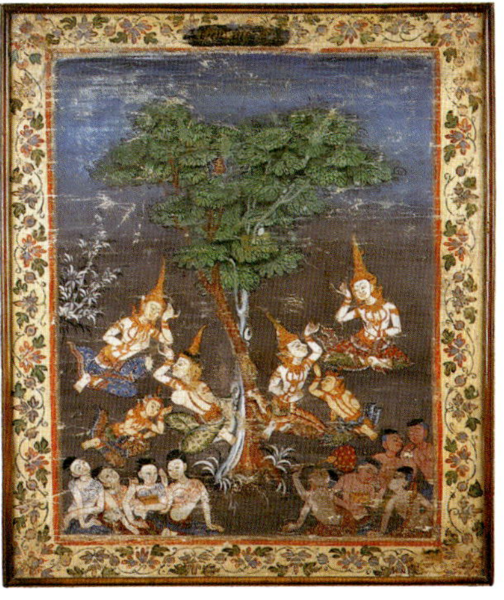

A scene from the Vessantara Jataka on cloth, showing Prince Vessantara and his family pausing for a rest on their way into exile. Dating from the early 19th-century Bangkok period, this is part of a set of 13 paintings.

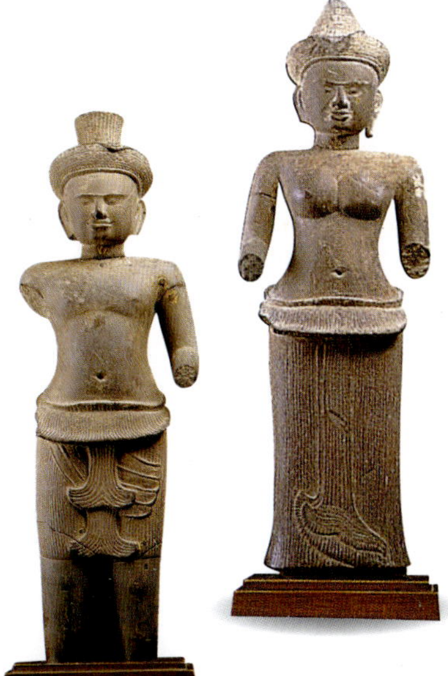

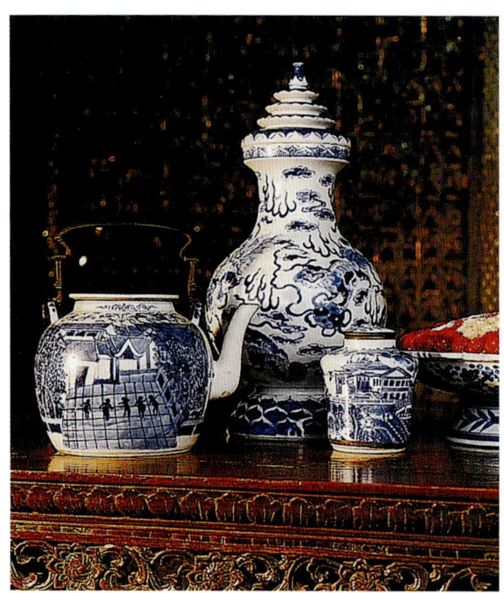

Above: Items from the collection of blue-and-white Chinese porcelain; some of these were made exclusively for export to Thailand, probably by order of the royal palace in the mid-19th century.

Below center: Carved wooden panel beneath one of the windows, decorated with a floral motif.

The Dining Room

The dining room of the Jim Thompson house, the scene of so many memorable entertainments during his life there, was originally part of a structure found in the village of Pak Hai on the Chao Phraya River. The two carved tables were made for gaming in the latter part of the nineteenth century and bear the insignia of King Chulalongkorn (1868-1910), while the chairs are covered with Thai silk. The crystal chandelier came from an old Bangkok palace of the same period, when Western-style decorations were popular with more affluent Thais.

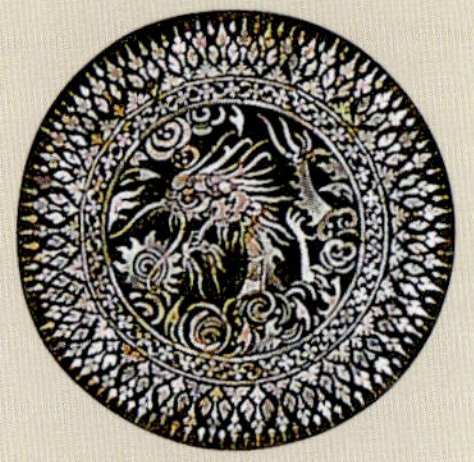

Detail from an inlaid mother-of-pearl design on a table. This art form came from China and reached a peak of perfection during the Ayutthaya period.

A number of the blue-and-white Chinese export porcelains displayed in this room came from Ayutthaya, a major trading center for such goods between the fifteenth and seventeenth centuries; a sunken ship found in the river near the old capital in the 1960s,

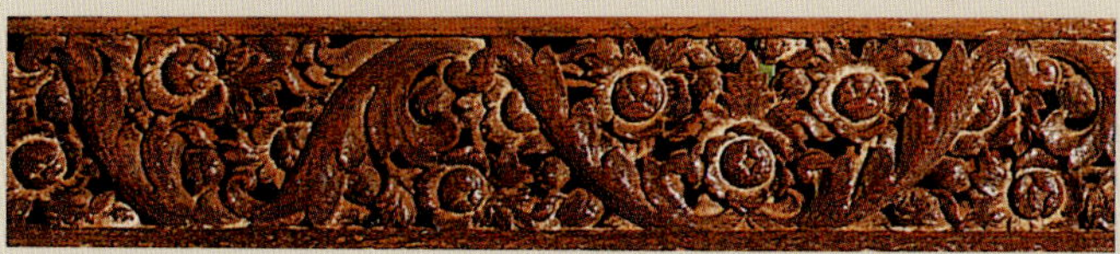

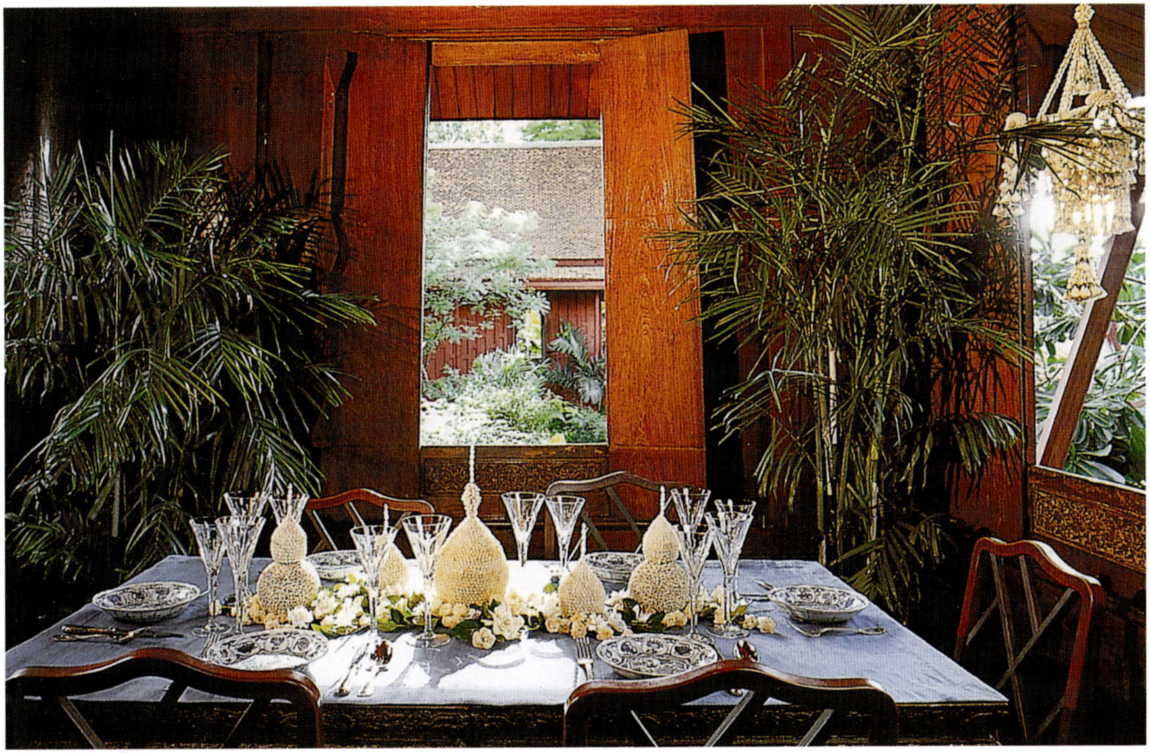

Above: The dining table set for a party; the plates are 17th-century blue-and-white Chinese ware.

Right: Annamese pieces, dating from the 14th-15th centuries, differ from Chinese blue-and-white ware as the bottom of the base is dark brown instead of white.

for example, contained nearly a thousand pieces of the ware. Some of the larger items were acquired from Indonesia and the Philippines. Among the other decorations in the room are carved altar tables and traditional paintings on cloth illustrating scenes from the Jataka stories.

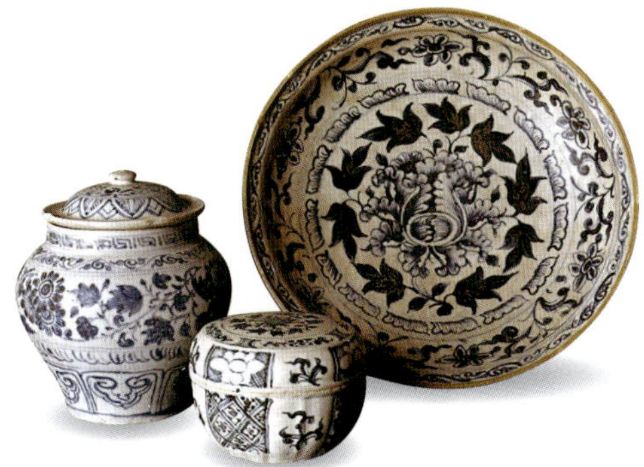

Center: The drawing room. All the furniture is Thai, while the figures displayed in the niches are Burmese.

Below: Gilded wooden figure of a *hong*, a mythological bird often associated with royalty in Thailand; early Bangkok School.

The Drawing Room

In both size and elegance, the drawing room is the most impressive part of the Jim Thompson house. The building dates from about 1800 and Thompson had long admired it on the daily visits he made to the weaving village of Bang Krua across the Klong Maha Nag canal. Partitioned into a number of small rooms by the 1950s, the structure was jointly owned by five heirs, each of whom wanted a home of his own. It was taken down and reassembled on the new site, the walls being reversed so that the carved panels under the windows faced inside; four of the side windows became niches in which to display objects.

The wooden figures displayed in the drawing room niches represent some of the lotus-bearing divinities attached to the doors of Burmese temples; they came from Amarapura and were given to Thompson as a gift when he went in the 1950s to advise the Burmese government on development of a silk industry.

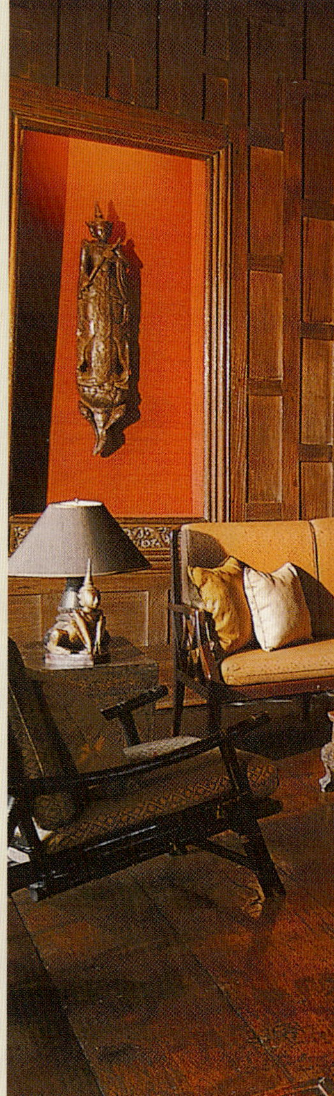

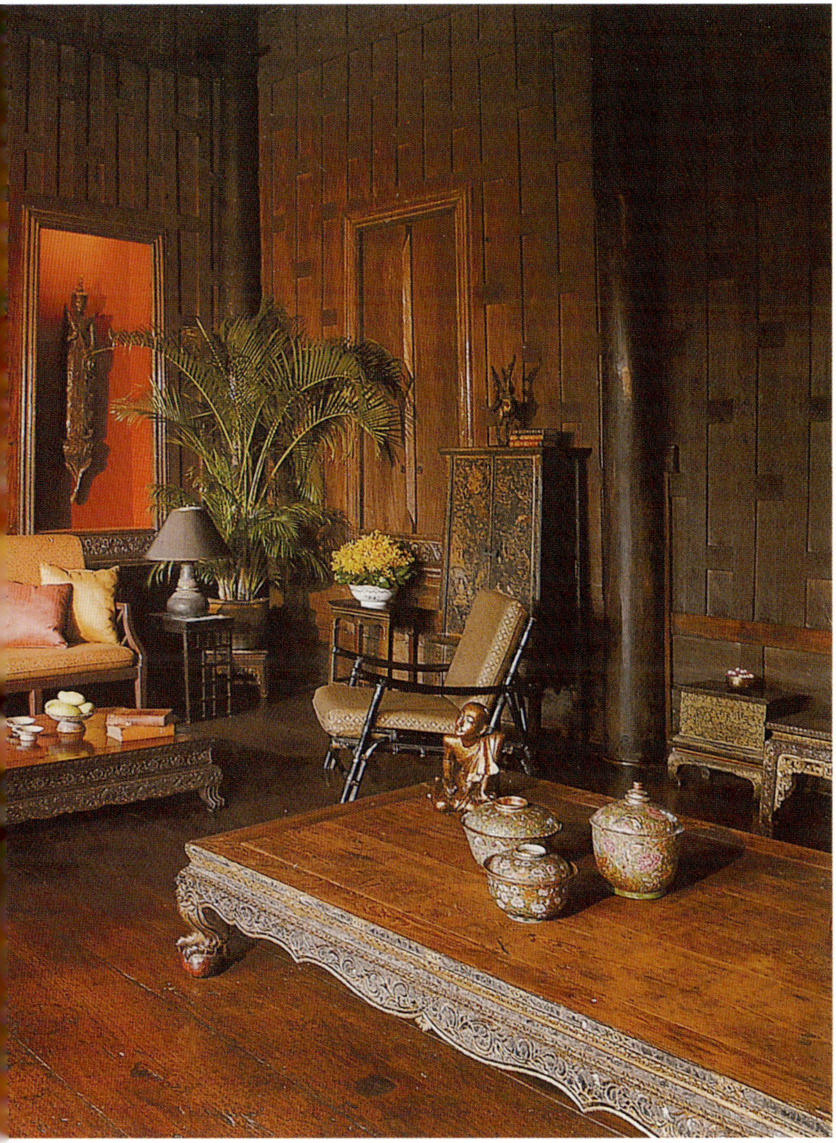

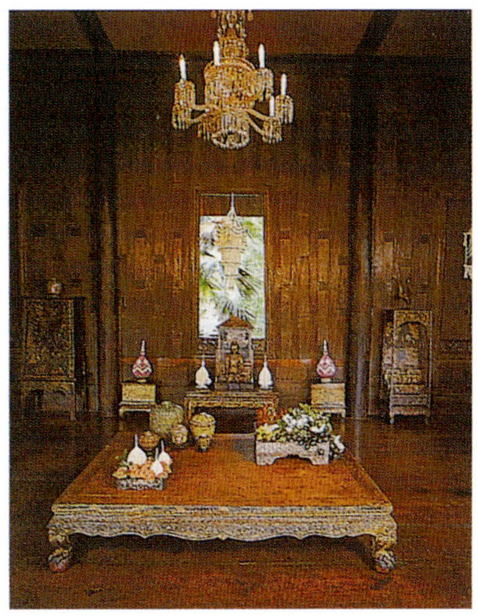

Above: In front of the window is placed a seated Burmese Buddha.

Below: Sandstone head of a Buddha image of the Ayutthaya School, U-Thong Style, late 13th century, 44.5 cm tall, it was found in Singhburi Province.

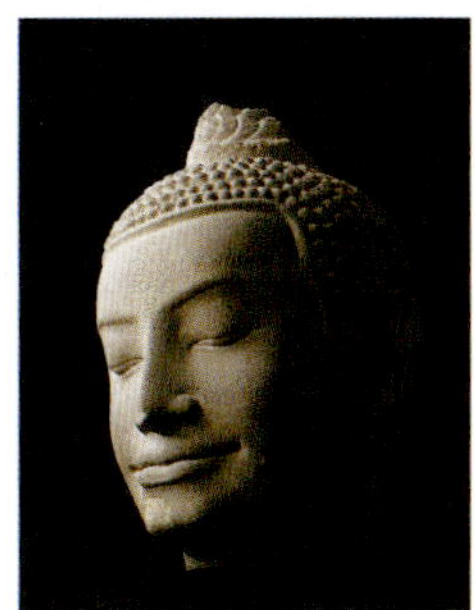

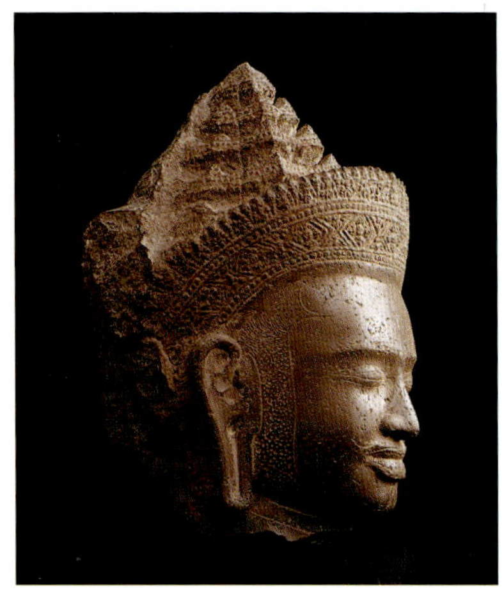

Above: Limestone head of a deity, that is half male (Siva) and half female (Uma), 36.5 cm tall, Lopburi school, 10th century.

Below right: Bronze halo, probably displayed as a backstand for a divinity, Lopburi school, 12th to 13th century.

The drawing room used to be decorated with bencharong which are now displayed in a special room. Bencharong, a term derived from Sanskrit that literally means "five colors", is a multi-colored overglaze enamel ware. Beginning in the Ayutthaya period and continuing into the late nineteenth century, these pentachromatic porcelains were made in China exclusively for export to Thailand, at first limited to members of the royal family. Earlier pieces have traditional designs which were supplied by Thai artists, though Chinese motifs became popular later.

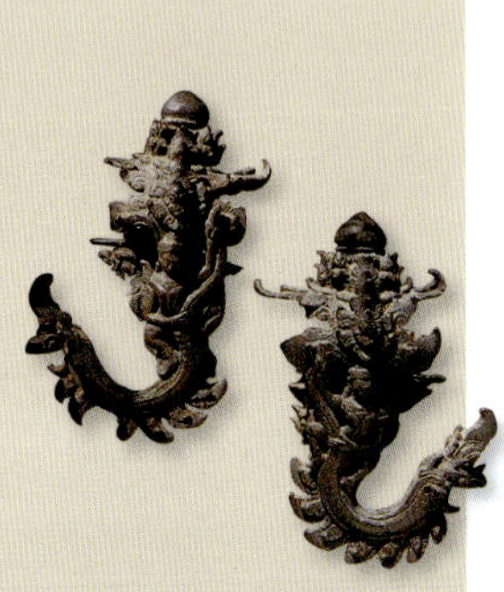

Bronze hooks from a palanquin, 19 cm tall, Lopburi school, 13th century.

In the center of the room is an old carved Thai bed with Chinese-style legs, while against the far wall is a cabinet made to hold religious scriptures and adorned with gold-and-black lacquer paintings. The gilded Buddha image on the low table below the window is Burmese, as are the two kneeling priests on the bed. The large crystal chandelier, like that in the dining room, was originally part of the decorations of a nineteenth-century Bangkok palace.

The partition doors dividing the drawing room from the master bedroom wing are the only non-Thai part of the house. They were originally the entrance to a pawnshop in the Chinese district of Bangkok. In the niches are Khmer bronze items dating from the tenth to thirteenth centuries; among them are parts of a palanquin and the tops of battle standards. Old cabinets and painted wooden figures from Burma are also displayed in this area.

One side of the room is open to views of the garden and a terrace paved with seventeenth-century brick from Ayutthaya. These are surrounded by a parapet into which have been set green glazed tiles that probably came to Thailand as ballast on rice boats returning from trade in China. Beyond the terrace is a traditional Thai *sala*, or pavilion.

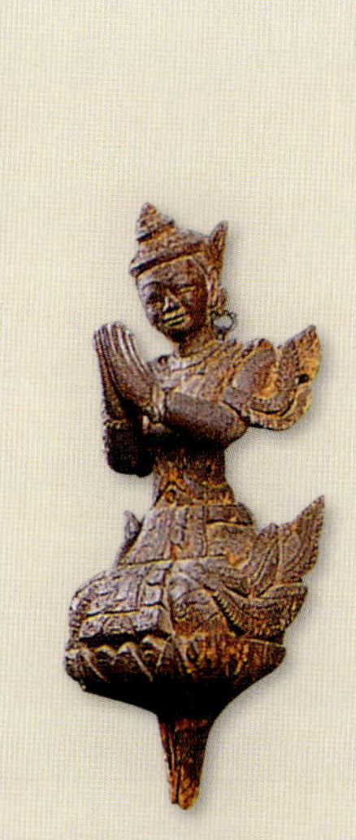

Above: Wooden divinity in an attitude of reverence.

Below: Manuscript illustration on paper, showing dancers in a type of Thai classical dance known as Lakhon Nai, performed only by women in the royal palace.

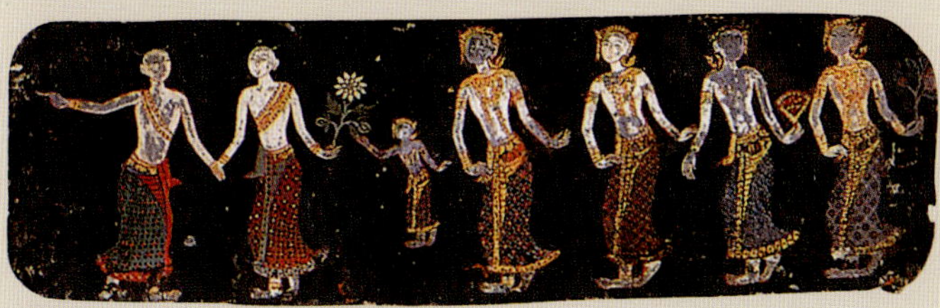

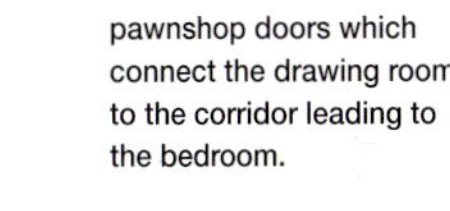

Below: The Chinese pawnshop doors which connect the drawing room to the corridor leading to the bedroom.

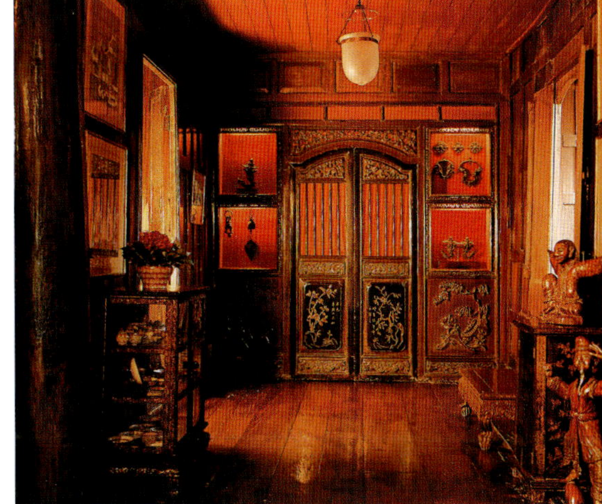

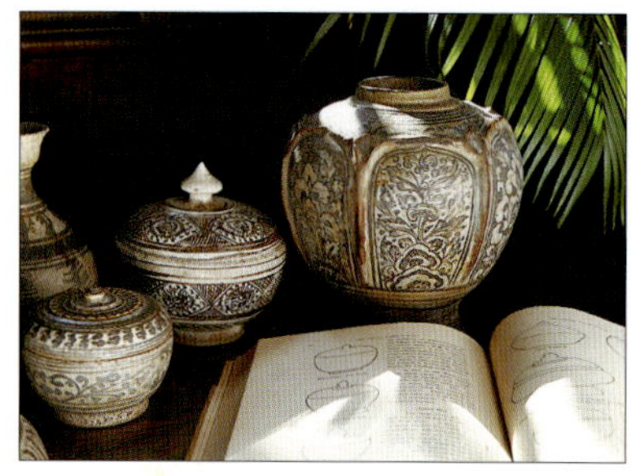

Above: Jars and covered containers made at Sawankhalok, a satellite city of the first Thai capital of Sukhothai, in the fourteenth and fifteenth centuries.

Below: Seated bronze Buddha, 20 cm tall, Lopburi school, 13th to 14th century. The image is in royal attire and in the gesture of calling the earth to witness.

The Study

The only air-conditioned space in the original house, this is the room where Jim Thompson read and wrote letters. The most prominent object on display, which some consider the most beautiful in the entire collection, is a standing limestone Buddha image of the early Dvaravati School dating from the eighth century; 104 cm high, it came from Lopburi province.

On the desk is a sandstone bas-relief carving of the Buddha holding a fan while preaching a sermon to his mother, flanked by two disciples in positions of reverence; it is of the Ayutthaya School. Also displayed is a selection of Thai ceramics made in kilns around Sukhothai, the first Thai capital, in the late fourteenth and fifteenth centuries; such wares were made principally for export and have been found in both Indonesia and the Philippines.

On the walls of the study are several European prints made as a consequence of a French embassy to the Ayutthaya court towards the end of the seventeenth century.

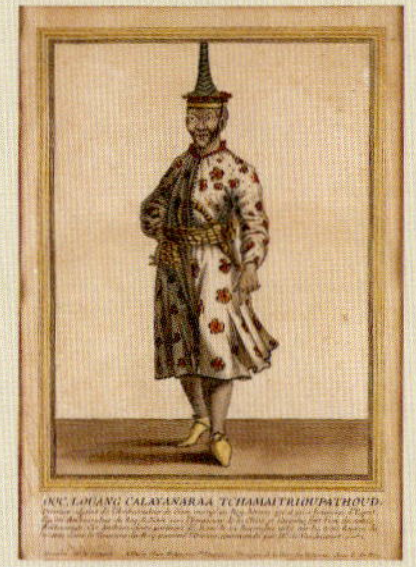

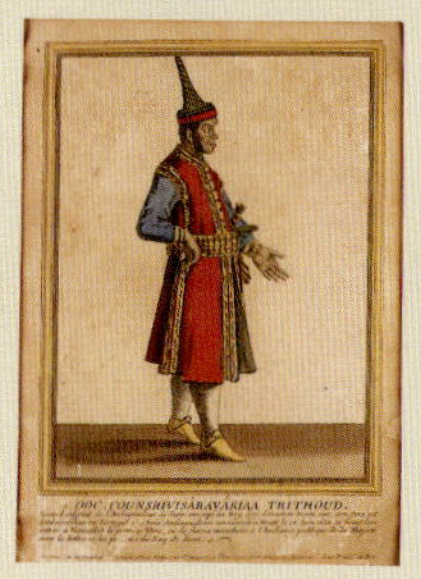

Two somewhat imaginative French prints depicting mandarins of the Siamese court, used to illustrate one of the memoirs written by a member of Louis XIV's embassy to Ayutthaya.

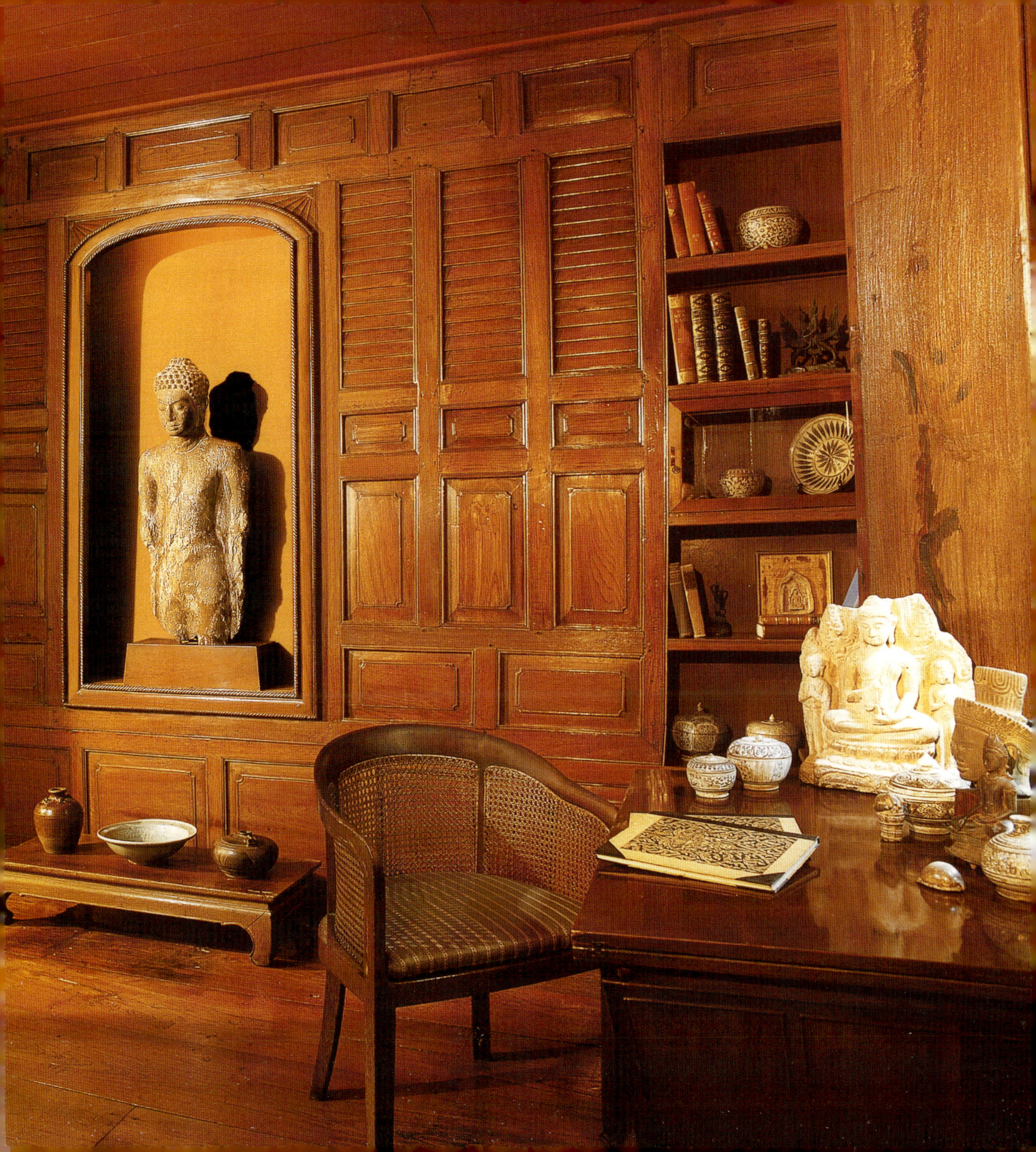

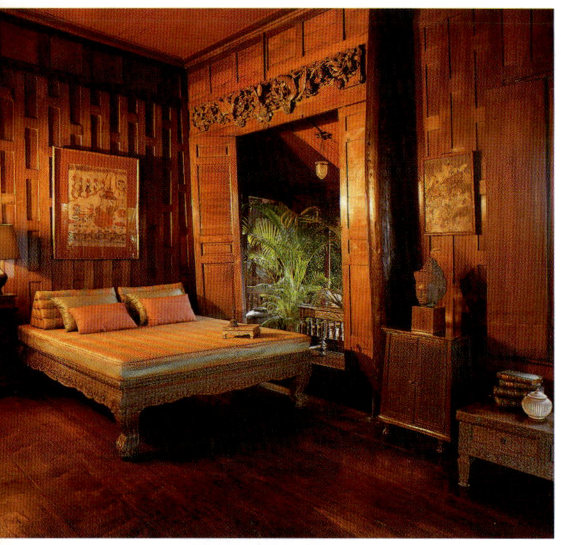

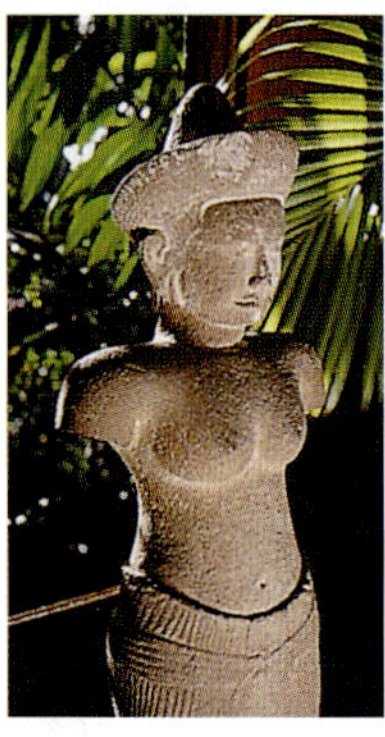

Above: An 11th-century standing figure of Uma in sandstone, 83.5 cm tall, Lopburi School; found in Thailand in the northeastern province of Khorat.

The Bedroom

The bedroom of Thompson's house has views of the terrace, the jungle-like tropical garden, and Klong Maha Nag, which Thompson crossed every morning to visit his silk weavers; doors also open onto a small verandah which in turn leads to a private guest wing added several years later.

Now displayed in the room are a number of fine Khmer pieces found in Thailand. These include a tenth-century limestone head of Ardhanari, a Hindu deity that is half-male (Siva) and half-female (Uma), in the style of Koh Ker, Cambodia; and a twelfth-century sandstone figure of Vishnu from Surin province.

Among the furnishings in the room are a carved teak bed with Thai silk covering, a scripture cabinet, a mice house, and an altar table with inlaid mother-of-pearl decorations. The painting above the bed in the upper left picture shows a scene from the Vessantara Jataka and differs from most of the others in that it is on handmade mulberry paper (*koi*) instead of cloth.

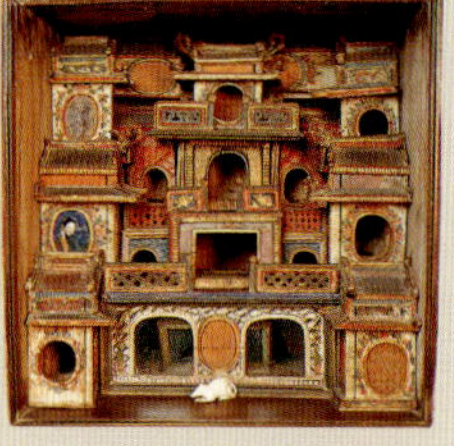

Above: A wooden maze for pet mice, 54 cm square, made by Chinese artisans in early 19th-century Bangkok. This inspired one of Thompson's visitors to write a children's book entitled *The Mouse House*.

Right: A fine torso of Buddha in grey limestone, Dvaravati School, 7th-8th century, from Lopburi region, 1.5 metres high. Wearing monastic dress, the Buddha held a fold of the robe in his hand. By virtue of its early date and artistic quality, this torso figures among the most important Dvaravati sculptures.

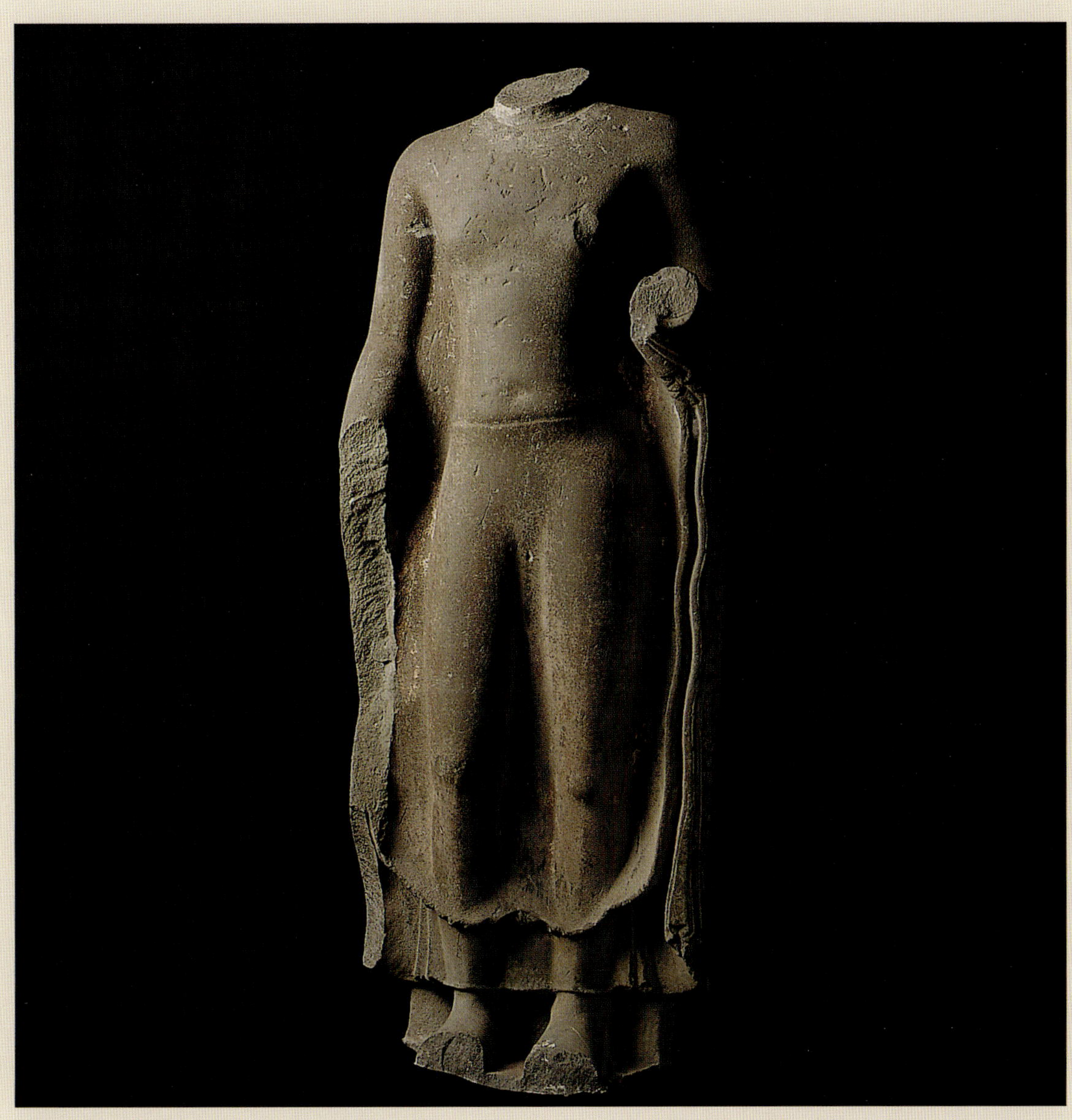

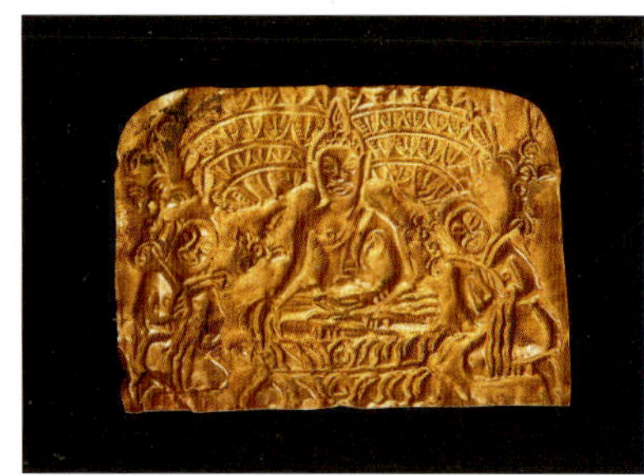

Above: Gold votive plaque, 15th-16th century. This plaque shows the Buddha together with two attendants seated under the sacred bodhi tree.

Below right: This votive plaque is in the Si-Tep School and dates back to the 8th-9th century. This piece contains a Sanskrit inscription and was found in Petchaboon province.

Below left: Gold votive plaque, Si-Tep School (8th-9th century). The figure depicted here is the Bodhisattva Maitreya.

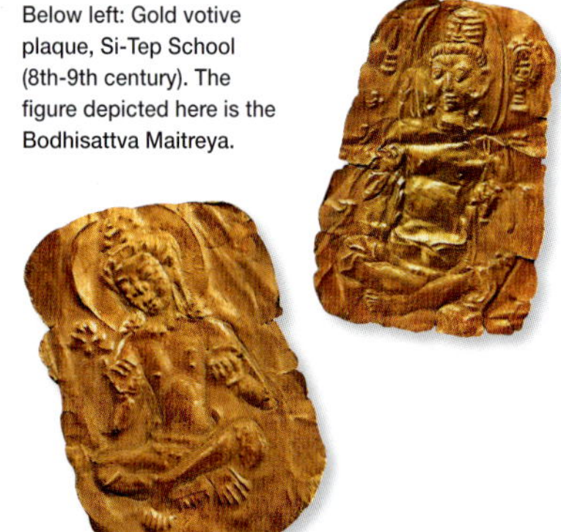

A Historical Overview of Styles

Thailand could well be described as a crossroads of Southeast Asian civilizations. Her geographical and political situation has allowed her to bring together a great diversity of schools of art. These can be set in two broad periods: one extends from the beginnings of Indianization in the 1st century AD to the first Thai kingdoms in the 13th century; the other begins from that date and runs on to the present. In the first period, Thailand received a great deal from beyond her borders, her role being an intermediary absorbing and diffusing these influences from and to other kingdoms; then, little by little, she developed her own form of art. The religious background is summed up remarkably well in these few lines written by Professor Jean Boisselier: 'Despite the complexities of political history, one can accept that the dominant trait of Thailand is her fidelity to the Buddhist faith, which provides continuity, a constant link binding together the most diverse tendencies in the course of the centuries.'

The collection contains a number of sculptures which can be categorized according to the chronology of seven schools proposed by H.R.H. Prince Damrong Rajanubhab, founder of Thai archaeology:

Dvaravati	7-11th C.
Srivijaya	8-13th C.
Lopburi (This designation includes all works of art of Khmer tradition discovered in Thailand)	7-14th C.
Sukhothai	13-15th C.
Lan Na	13-20th C.
Ayutthaya	14-18th C.
Bangkok (Ratanakosin)	18-20th C.

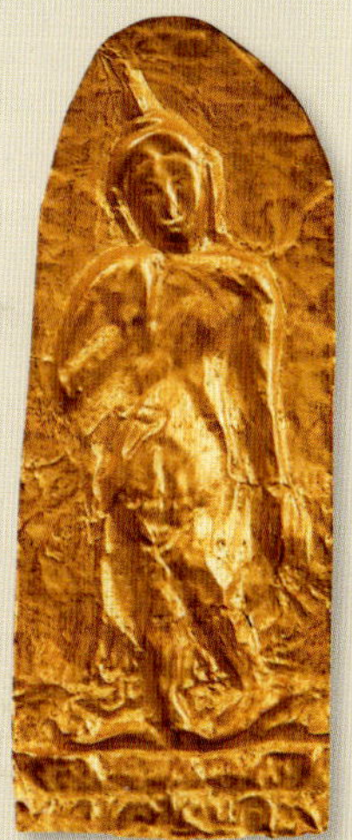

This gold votive plaque depicts a walking Buddha with the distinctive Sukhothai features. Sukhothai School, 14th to 15th century.